Fantasy Chronicles

MERMAIDS AND MERMEN

Shannon Knudsen

Lerner Publications Company · Minneapolis

Lerner Publications Company
A division of Lerner Publishing Group, Inc.
241 First Avenue North
Minneapolis, MN 55401 U.S.A.

Website address: www.lernerbooks.com

Library of Congress Cataloging-in-Publication Data

Knudsen, Shannon, 1971–
        Mermaids and mermen / by Shannon Knudsen.
            p.   cm. — (Fantasy chronicles)
        Includes bibliographical references and index.
        ISBN 978–0–8225–9981–4 (lib. bdg. : alk. paper)
        1. Mermaids—Juvenile literature. 2. Mermen—Juvenile literature. I. Title.
    GR910.K57 2010
    398.21—dc22   2009009960

Manufactured in the United States of America
1 2 3 4 5 6 – BP – 15 14 13 12 11 10

TABLE OF CONTENTS

CHAPTER 1

THE MANY CHARMS OF MERFOLK

You're walking along the beach when the singing starts. You've never heard anything so beautiful. Before you even think about it, you're walking toward the sound. The moon casts a clear, eerie glow over the water. Waves crash against the shore. The sandy ground becomes rockier, and you almost lose your footing.

Then you see her. A young woman, sitting on a rock out in the water. As she sings, she combs her long, dark hair. Her song makes you think of every possible good thing: The best day you've ever had. The best food you've ever tasted. The best gift you've ever gotten.

You walk out into the water toward the woman. It's quite cold. You realize you've left your shoes on, but it seems silly to turn back now that they're already soaked. Soon the water is deep enough to swim in. The next time you look up toward the singing woman, she's still on the rock. Yet she seems farther away than before. Your eyes must be playing tricks on you.

You keep swimming. You start to feel tired, but the song lures you on. And then there she is, right in front of you. She reaches for your hand. By the time you realize that she has a huge, scaly tail where her legs should be, she's pulling you down, down, into the murky deep. You can't seem to let go or swim away.

Your lungs start to fill with water. You've been fooled by a mermaid, and she will never, ever let you go.

Secrets from the Deep

Water has always played a huge part in our lives. We need it to live, grow crops, raise animals, and catch fish. So it's no surprise that every successful and long-lasting civilization in human history has been located close to water.

But water is also dangerous. The sea, large lakes, and deep rivers seem powerful and beyond our control. Storms sink our ships and drown us. Sharks, alligators, and other water-dwelling animals may attack us or even kill us. Living with water means living with the possibility of death. Maybe that's why people have always told stories about strange and frightening aquatic creatures.

A storm like this one could mean death for sailors, especially in fragile wooden ships like these. A Dutch artist painted this picture in 1876.

Lots of those stories are about merfolk—beings that are part human and part fish. In the English language, female merfolk are traditionally called mermaids. Males are called mermen. They have many other names as well.

Merfolk certainly aren't all alike. Yet many merfolk stories have similar details, even in very different cultures. Almost all types of merfolk have the upper body of a human and the lower body and tail of a large fish. (Some merfolk have a split tail with two branches.) Mermaids often have long hair and beautiful faces. They sit on rocks or float at the surface of the water, combing their hair and singing. Their voices are lovelier than any human's. Mermen, on the other hand, are often ugly. They aren't especially musical, either. Both mermaids and mermen can be kind to humans, but in ancient stories, they're more likely to cause trouble. Mermaids are known for luring men into the water and drowning them, for example.

A mermaid swims toward the surface in this computer image. Many stories describe merfolk as being able to breathe in both air and water.

THE MANY CHARMS OF MERFOLK

Why do these features appear in stories from cultures as far apart as South America and Europe? People who study the past think that sailors, merchants, and explorers carried folktales from place to place as they traveled. Over time, as people from different lands traded stories, the tales began to become more alike.

But where do merfolk stories come from to start with? Who came up with the idea of a creature that's half person and half fish? And why?

Worth Paying For?

Scientists all around the world are convinced that mermaids and mermen aren't real, but many people continue to believe in merfolk sightings. Just ask the security guards at the Silliman University Institute of Environmental and Marine Sciences. This laboratory is in Dumaguete, a city in the Philippines. In February 2009, radio stations in the city announced that a mermaid had been found nearby. A rumor started that she had been taken to the lab for study. Dozens of people came to the lab to see her. The guards explained that there was no mermaid at all. But the crowd insisted on paying for tickets to enter the lab and find out for themselves!

Some scholars think that the people who first believed they saw such creatures actually saw something else. For example, manatees are ocean mammals that have a shape somewhat like a human's. Walruses and seals do as well. Perhaps sailors who had been at sea for weeks or months mistook these animals for merfolk. Whatever the case, our folklore is full of incredible stories as a result.

Sailors might have mistaken manatees for mermaids when these curious animals swam up to look at a ship.

THE MANY CHARMS
OF MERFOLK

CHAPTER 2

European Merfolk

Some of the oldest examples of merfolk can be found in the mythology of ancient Greece. Greek myths date back more than three thousand years. The Greek god Triton was a merman. His father was Poseidon, the god of the sea. Triton's mother, Amphitrite, was a nature spirit known as a nymph. Triton carried a three-pronged weapon called a trident. He also had a conch shell that he could blow like a horn. It sounded so loud that it could scare away a giant. In case that wasn't enough, the conch had the power to create fierce waves or to calm the water.

Over time, Greek writers started to use Triton's name to describe mermen in general. The tritons were said to have green hair, scales, gills beneath their ears, and a tail like a dolphin's. Like the original Triton, they carried conch shells. The tritons acted as escorts to Poseidon, blowing into their shells to announce the god's arrival. They also used the shells to raise or calm waves, depending on Poseidon's wishes. Another job of the tritons was to pull the chariot of Aphrodite, the goddess of love, when she traveled across the ocean.

The Song of the Sirens

In the myths of ancient Greece, many sailors met their death when they heard the song of the Sirens. These creatures were half bird and half woman. Their song was so sweet that no human could resist it. But ships that steered toward the singing would be wrecked on the rocky shores where the Sirens lived.

Over time, storytellers started to link the beautiful voices of the Sirens with the singing of mermaids. That's why Sirens are sometimes portrayed as mermaids rather than bird-women. But either way, you wouldn't want to meet them without a good pair of earplugs!

Merrows and Mermaids

Great Britain and Ireland are nations in northwestern Europe. They are both surrounded by water. Maybe that's why they're home to so many mermaid legends. A very old legend comes from Scotland, which is part of Britain. It appears in the *Annals of the Four Masters*, a book of history. According to the monks who wrote the book, a mermaid washed up on the shore of Scotland in A.D. 887. She was 195 feet (59 meters) long, more than half the length of a modern football field. Each of her fingers measured 7 feet (2 m), longer

than a very tall adult human. Her nose was about the same size, which meant that each of her nostrils was big enough for a person to sleep inside!

Ireland also has its own kind of merfolk, called merrows. Both female and male merrows have green hair and fish tails, with the upper body of a human. All merrows wear a red cap, which gives them the power to swim deep in the ocean. But female merrows are

In this English illustration from the 1200s, mermaids sing to sailors. If the sailors were to fall asleep to the sound, their ship would wreck.

beautiful to human beings, while the males are horribly ugly. The males have pig faces, green skin, and bright red noses.

Male and female merrows also behave differently. Female merrows sometimes fall in love with humans. They even marry them and have families. (The children of a merrow and a human are said to be born with webbed fingers, webbed toes, and scales.) Male merrows are friendly jokers, but they have a darker side. They like to collect the souls of drowned fishers. The merrows store the souls in cages in their undersea homes.

Strange Friends

An old Irish tale tells about a human named Jack who made friends with a merrow named Coomara. Coomara had an extra red cap, and he invited Jack to borrow it and visit him under the sea. Jack agreed. He clung to Coomara's tail as the merrow swam deep below the ocean. Jack was certain he would drown. But suddenly they reached the ocean floor, and Jack could breathe again. When he looked up, he saw that the water ended far above them, like an undersea sky.

This carving of a mermaid appears on a stone arch inside an Irish church built in the 1400s.

The Seal People

A Scottish water being, the selkie, has an amazing power. Most of the time, selkies look like seals. But a selkie can come onto shore and remove its sealskin. Then it becomes human until it puts the skin on again. Both male and female selkies are very attractive. Sometimes humans fall in love with them. Many stories tell of a human stealing the sealskin of a female selkie, trapping her in human form. A selkie who was caught this way often married her captor and had a family with him. But if she ever found her sealskin, she would rush back to the ocean, put the skin on, and vanish into the water for good.

Fishers and sailors believed that if the blood of a selkie was shed in the water, a terrible storm would follow. This belief, along with other selkie stories, spread from Scotland into Ireland and other parts of northern Europe.

Seals rest on the shore of a Scottish island.

Many stories about merfolk come from fishers who live along these rocky shores in Ireland.

The man and the merrow had a wonderful dinner of fish. Coomara showed Jack his collection of treasures from the ocean. Much to Jack's distress, the merrow had a long row of soul cages. Coomara said he figured that the souls of the drowned were happy to be in his warm, dry home. But Jack put his head near one of the cages and listened. He heard a sobbing sound.

Back at home, Jack made a plan. Coomara had taken back his extra red cap. So Jack invited Coomara to his house and gave him so much alcohol to drink that the merrow became drunk. Soon he passed out. Jack snatched the cap Coomara wore and hurried to the house at the bottom of the sea. He took each soul cage out of the house, opened it to let the soul escape, and put the cage back just where he'd found it. Then he rushed home, where he found the merrow still snoring.

Coomara never noticed that his soul cages had been emptied. Every now and then, Jack played the same trick. That way he could free any souls that Coomara had caught since Jack's last rescue mission. And the merrow and the man stayed friends for years.

Another story of a strange friendship comes from northern England. A fisherman named Lutey found a mermaid on the beach. She had been washed into a pool among the rocks by the high tide. When the tide went down, the mermaid was left in the pool, trapped until the next high tide. Lutey agreed to carry the mermaid back to the sea. In return, she granted him three wishes. He asked for the power to break evil spells. Then he asked for the power to make spirits do good acts. Finally, he asked for these powers to be given to his family as well, for all time.

Merfolk Farmers

Some merfolk kept farm animals, just as the people who told stories about them did. A mermaid of Wales called Gwenhidwy was a shepherdess. It was said that the foamy white crests of sea waves were Gwenhidwy's flock of sheep. And mermaids from Denmark known as *havfrue* were said to drive herds of white cattle along the shore to eat plants.

The mermaid liked that Lutey asked for such unselfish things. She gave him another present—her comb. She explained that he would always be able to summon her with it. Then, as they reached the water, she did something surprising. Instead of saying good-bye, she tried to lure Lutey under the waves along with her. She was so beautiful that he would have gone with her. But just in time, his dog howled from shore. Lutey looked up and saw the cottage where his family lived. He pulled away and waved his knife at the mermaid. She let him escape but told him that she would return for him in nine years.

A mermaid combs her hair in a 1900 painting by British artist John William Waterhouse.

Sure enough, nine years later, Lutey was out on a boat with his son. A beautiful woman appeared in the water. Lutey plunged into the surf and was never seen again.

The Tale of Melusine

A famous legend from France stars a water fairy named Melusine. This haunting story has been told and retold by many writers, so there are many versions. As the result of a curse, Melusine turns into a mermaid one day each week. (In some Melusine stories, she has the tail of a serpent rather than a fish. Sometimes she has wings too.) She marries a human man who doesn't realize that she's a part-time mermaid. Melusine makes her new husband promise to leave her alone all day every Saturday. Her husband keeps the promise for years. But at last, he grows so curious that he peeks through Melusine's keyhole one Saturday. Imagine his surprise when he sees that his beautiful wife is a fish from the waist down! Melusine knows that her husband has broken his promise. She leaves him forever.

Melusine's husband discovers her secret in an 1844 painting by a German artist.

EUROPEAN MERFOLK

CHAPTER 3

AROUND THE WORLD

Many old merfolk stories come from Europe. But they're certainly not the only ones. Across every ocean, you'll find examples that people have shared for generations.

North America has plenty of merfolk, for example. Eastern Canada is home to the Mi'kmaq, a Native American people. They tell of the Halfway People, whose upper bodies are human and lower bodies are shaped like those of fish. The Halfway People don't lure victims into the water or drown them. In fact, they do favors for fishers by singing to warn them of coming storms. But if the fishermen act unkindly or disrespectfully, the Halfway People have the power to create huge storms that can overturn boats and send the people in them to a watery death.

At the other end of North America, in the Caribbean Sea, lies the island nation of Haiti. A Haitian folktale reveals the powers of a mermaid's charms. A group of men are sitting near the shore one day, playing dominoes and talking. Suddenly they notice a woman far out in the sea. She has long white hair and is unusually beautiful.

As the men watch her, one of their group gets up. He walks toward the woman, into the water. As he approaches, the woman seems to get farther away. The man keeps going, walking along the bottom of the sea. Soon the water covers his head, and he disappears.

The villagers are frightened by their friend's disappearance. For weeks, no one goes near the water. Then, after three months, the missing man returns. He explains that the strange woman was a mermaid. She took him to a lovely underwater city, where he was able to breathe. The man and the mermaid were happy together. But that morning, he awoke to find himself swimming at the surface of the ocean. The mermaid must have known that

A Haitian man
fixes his fishing
net on the shore.
People who live
and work by the
sea tell many
stories about its
mysteries.

he missed his home, the man figured. From then on, everyone in the village treated the mermaid's friend with great respect.

Merfolk Magic in South America

An old story from the country of Chile tells about a mermaid whose wits weren't quite as strong as her magic powers. A poor old fisherman couldn't catch any fish one day. He knew that if he failed to bring fish to the king, the king would cut off his head. At the end of the day, a mermaid appeared near the fisherman's boat. She made him an offer. She would give him a supply of fish if he made a promise in return. He would have to give her whatever came to meet him when he returned home, once that thing turned sixteen years old.

The fisherman was desperate. He felt certain his dog would meet him, so he agreed to the mermaid's offer. He cast his net and caught a huge amount of fish. But when he got home that night, his little son came out ahead of the dog! The fisherman would have to give up his son when the boy turned sixteen.

When the day came, his son told him not to worry. The son put a colorful saddle on the wildest horse they owned and went to the shore. The mermaid was enchanted by the saddle and the horse. She demanded them as well as the boy. The father tossed her the horse's rope. The mermaid pulled and pulled, but she couldn't drag the wild horse into the ocean. At last, the rope gave way. The boy rode for the hills as fast as he could.

After his escape, the boy lived a lucky life. He made friends with talking animals that gave him the power to change into their form. Then he married a princess. But one day, he returned to the sea-shore. The mermaid lured him underwater, and he was trapped.

Luckily, the princess was clever. She took three golden apples to the shore. The mermaid asked for them. The princess traded the apples for a look at her husband. When the mermaid lifted the princess's husband above the water, he used his animal power to change into a dove and fly away. He promised never to go to the beach again.

This story shows that no matter how powerful a being such as a mermaid might be, a clever human can be even more powerful. That must have been a great comfort to people who feared scary water spirits!

The Amazon River, the largest river in the world, runs through the South American country of Brazil. Storytellers in Brazil describe a special kind of dolphin that lives in the Amazon. It isn't a merman or a mermaid, but it has the power to transform into a human and then back to a dolphin again. These beings are called *encantados*. This Portuguese word means "enchanted ones." Encantados can be either female or male. Sometimes they visit human celebrations to enjoy the music and dancing. If they fall in love with a human, they may play tricks to win the person's love. Sometimes they even take on the shape of their beloved's wife or husband!

Another favorite activity of encantados is to lure humans to their underwater city, Encante. Sometimes these people are released after a while. Often, though, they remain in Encante forever. Over time, they slowly turn into encantados themselves.

Encantados also do favors for people. Some help canoes and boats reach safety during storms. Others fetch lost oars from the bottom of the Amazon. That's one reason that the people of the Amazon region make sure not to harm dolphins. Another is

Myths about the Amazon River dolphin *(above)* can cause problems. Some people kill these dolphins and sell their body parts as items with magical power.

that a person who wounds or kills an encantado in dolphin form may go blind or insane!

Asian Merfolk

The mermaids of Japan are called *ningyo*. Their bodies are huge and almost completely fishlike. Only the head is human. Sometimes a ningyo's head is beautiful, and sometimes not. But ningyo do tend to have beautiful spirits. These gentle beings warn people of storms and other dangers.

The Solomon Islands, a nation in the South Pacific Ocean, have been the home of Melanesian people for thousands of years. Their folklore tells of a frightening kind of merman called an *adaro.* An adaro has a mostly human body with fins that extend from his legs and feet. His head has ears and gills as well as a sharp, pointy spine in place of a nose. Adaros hate human beings and will kill any that enter the waters where they live. Their

A Chinese artist made this ceramic mermaid sometime in the 1000s.

main weapons are schools of poisonous flying fish, which travel along rainbows with them after storms.

A much kinder sort of merfolk can be found in the mythology of ancient Mesopotamia. (We know this area as Iraq.) The seven *abgal* looked like mermen and were known for their intelligence and goodwill toward humans. In fact, they were servants of Enki, the god of wisdom. During the day, the abgal came onto land and served as tutors for humankind. They shared their knowledge of science and the arts until nightfall. Then they returned to the sea.

WEIRD AND WEIRDER

What has arms, legs, a human face, a priest's robes, fish scales, and webbed feet? No real animal does, that's for sure. But in 1575, a Swiss naturalist named Konrad Gesner wrote about a bizarre creature that has these features. It was called a bishop-fish. Gesner had never seen one, but he believed the reports of people who claimed that they had. Gesner also described a monk-fish (right). It had a fish tail, fins instead of arms, scales, a monk's robe, and the shaved hairstyle that monks often wore.

An African Mermaid

In central and western Africa, people tell tales of a water spirit named Mami Wata. She is often portrayed as a mermaid who carries a snake. (Sometimes she looks like a human woman too.) People who study folktales think that Mami Wata stories may have begun when European traders and explorers brought mermaid stories to Africa. That might explain why she has fair skin and straight hair rather than the dark skin and curly hair of many African people.

Mami Wata is known for healing sick people. Sometimes she drowns people, though. Some believe that she sends back those she drowns. They return to Earth as her servants.

An artist paints a mural of Mami Wata (sometimes called Mami Water) in the western African country of Ghana

THE FEEJEE MERMAID

CHAPTER 4

FAKES AND FRAUDS

Some of the world's most interesting merfolk aren't from stories. They're so-called real mermaids that people created to fool other people. For hundreds of years in Europe, sailors made these fake mermaids to pass the time—and to fatten their wallets. Plenty of folks would trade a few coins for a tiny mermaid that a sailor claimed to have found in a faraway ocean.

The process of making a mermaid began with the dried-out body of a ray or a skate. These flat, odd-looking sea animals have strange shapes with interesting patches of color. The sailor would carve the body into a monsterlike creature. Sometimes pieces from another fish or animal body would be sewn on to create fins, tails, or wings. Finally, the carver applied varnish. When the varnish dried, the result looked like the dried body of an actual beast. Some of these fakes were shaped like dragons or demons. Many were mermaids.

Jenny Hanivers

This practice became so common that the carved mermaids were given their own name—Jenny Hanivers. Where did this strange name come from? Some people who study the history of language think it came from Antwerp, Belgium. That's where many of the first carvings were made. In French they were called *jeunes d'Anvers*. *Jeunes* is French for "young girls," while *d'Anvers* is French for "from Antwerp." So the name meant "little girls from Antwerp." British sailors repeated the French words in English, and the name Jenny Haniver was the result.

Most people who sold Jenny Hanivers probably made a few bucks. But a few clever crooks took the fake mermaid business to a new level. A sea captain named Samuel Barrett Eades found this out the hard way during the 1820s.

The Feejee Mermaid

Captain Eades commanded a merchant ship called the *Pickering*. In 1822 he sailed to the Dutch East Indies in Southeast Asia. (This area later became the nation of Indonesia.) There a group of merchants showed him an amazing thing. It was a small, dried-out crea-

This Jenny Haniver comes from Italy.

ture with an upper body like a human's and the lower body and tail of a fish.

Eades studied the creature carefully. He figured that if pieces of different animals had been sewn together to create it, he would find a seam between the tail and the upper body. But he found no seam at all. He became convinced that he was viewing the remains of an actual mermaid.

The merchants wanted a huge amount of money for their prize—five thousand dollars. Eades had no money at all. But he did have the *Pickering*—sort of. He owned one-eighth of the ship. His boss back in London owned the other seven-eighths. Still, Eades had to have the mermaid. He sold his ship without permission, bought the mysterious corpse, and set sail for home.

As you know by now, a few of the old mermaid stories have happy endings. But many don't. This one doesn't either. Back in London, Eades set up an exhibit of his mermaid. He charged people one shilling to look at her. At first, several hundred people came every day. Many scientists agreed that the mermaid was real. But then one of the greatest animal experts in Britain exposed

Eades hired an artist to make this drawing of his mermaid. The picture appeared in ads inviting people to see this curiosity.

the mermaid as a fake. William Clift could see that she had the head of an orangutan, the teeth of a baboon, and the tail of a fish, possibly a salmon. Her eyes and fingernails were artificial. She had been put together expertly, but she wasn't real.

London newspapers reported the truth about the mermaid, and people stopped paying to see her. Poor Eades found himself in debt. He still had to pay back the owner of the *Pickering* for the cost of the ship. A court ordered him to work for the ship's owner for free. Eades sailed without pay for twenty years, until he died.

What about the fake mermaid? She ended up in the United States. The captain's son sold her to a museum manager. She ended up on exhibit again, this time by the famous showman P. T.

Barnum. He called her the Feejee Mermaid, saying she had been caught off the Fiji Islands in the South Pacific Ocean. Eventually, the mermaid disappeared. But she wasn't the last of her kind. Fake mermaids kept showing up throughout the nineteenth century and beyond.

THE MERMAID'S PURSE

If someone comes up to you on a beach and shows you something called a mermaid's purse, you shouldn't suspect a fraud. Mermaid's purses aren't actually the handbags of merfolk, but they're real. These small, dark-colored objects look like sealed pouches. They're the egg cases of sharks, rays, and skates. Inside each mermaid's purse is the egg of one of these ocean animals. If a purse remains in the water long enough, the egg inside it will grow. Once the egg has developed enough, it hatches from the purse. A baby shark, ray, or skate swims forth into the sea. But egg cases often wash up on shore before they hatch. Some clever beachcomber must have come up with the idea of the mermaid's purse long ago, and the name stuck.

CHAPTER 5

THE ENTERTAINING MERFOLK

One story has probably had the biggest influence on how we view merfolk in the twenty-first century. It goes all the way back to 1836. That's when the Danish author Hans Christian

Andersen wrote "The Little Mermaid." This fairy tale has inspired films, TV shows, games, toys, a Broadway play, and a ballet. Andersen wrote his story as a fairy tale for children, but most modern kids never read it or hear it. That's because they usually see Disney's 1989 movie instead. But the two stories are actually quite different.

In the Disney movie, the little mermaid is named Ariel. But in Andersen's tale, she has no name. Like Ariel, Andersen's mermaid falls in love with a handsome prince and saves him from drowning. Both mermaids agree to give the sea witch their voice in exchange for legs. The sea witch takes Ariel's voice magically. But Andersen's mermaid isn't so lucky. The witch cuts out her tongue.

The little mermaid's suffering doesn't end there. Every step she takes on her new legs feels as if she's walking on knives. Even worse, the prince thinks a different girl saved him. He loves that girl, not the mermaid. Then his parents arrange for him to marry a princess. She turns out to be the very girl the prince already loves!

The mermaid knows that the prince's marriage will mean her death. The sea witch promised her that on the morning after his wedding to another, the mermaid would dissolve into sea foam. Right before sunrise, her sisters arrive with a knife. If the little mermaid kills the prince before morning, she'll live. But she can't bear to destroy the person she loves. She gives up and plunges into the sea.

Instead of dying, the little mermaid discovers that her goodness has earned her a place among the daughters of the air. If she continues to do good deeds for three hundred years, she will earn a soul. In that way, she can live forever.

This famous statue of the Little Mermaid sits on a rock in the harbor of Copenhagen, Denmark, where Hans Christian Andersen spent most of his life.

If you've seen Disney's *The Little Mermaid,* you already know that things turn out very differently for Ariel. Maybe Andersen didn't think fairy tales should have happy endings. Or maybe the moviemakers at Disney didn't think modern viewers would want to see such a sad movie! Still, Disney's movie features two interesting merfolk besides Ariel. Her father, King Triton, is named for the Greek sea god. He carries a trident, just like the original Triton did. The sea witch, Ursula, is a twisted sort of merfolk too. She has the upper body of a woman and the lower body of a squid.

A Mermaid Named Madison

Five years before Ariel made it to the big screen, the 1984 movie *Splash* helped bring mermaids to life for modern audiences. Tom Hanks stars as Allen, a man who was saved from drowning by a mermaid when he was a boy. Allen thinks that his boyhood adventure was just his imagination. Still, his feelings for the mermaid are so strong that no human woman can capture his heart.

Tom Hanks stars opposite Daryl Hannah, who plays a mermaid, in the 1984 film *Splash*.

Then an amazing thing happens. The mermaid saves Allen from drowning again. She leaves him on the beach and returns to the water. There she finds the wallet Allen had dropped. Because her tail turns into legs when it's dry, the mermaid is able to walk. She swims ashore in New York City and uses the wallet to track down Allen. They fall in love immediately.

Like many mermaids of legend, this one has a hard time pretending to be human. She has no name, a problem that she solves by taking the name Madison from a street sign. Although her tail turns into legs when it's dry, she must wet it frequently in the bathtub. That turns her into a mermaid again! Before long, Allen finds out that Madison isn't a woman after all. Even worse, scientists are chasing her so that they can study her in a laboratory. Will Madison and her new romance survive?

The old story of the lovelorn mermaid gets a twist in Alice Hoffman's 2002 book *Aquamarine.* Two human girls, Claire and Hailey, have one more summer together before Claire has to move away. They spend as much time as they can at their favorite place, the beach club. One night, a huge storm washes jellyfish and seaweed into the club's swimming pool. The girls find a mermaid hidden beneath the tangled mess. The sharp-tongued creature tells them that her name is Aquamarine.

Claire and Hailey want to return Aquamarine to the ocean, but she has other ideas. She's fallen in love with Raymond, the cute guy who works at the snack bar. Even though she's dying, Aquamarine refuses to go home until she can win Raymond's heart. The girls must arrange a date, disguise Aquamarine's tail, and figure out how to conceal the fact that she can't walk. *Aquamarine* was made into a movie in 2006, starring Sara Paxton as the mermaid.

Sara Paxton stars as the mermaid Aquamarine in the 2006 film of the same name.

Merfolk Mysteries

If you're not a fan of mermaid romance, don't worry. There are plenty of ways to experience the wonders of merfolk and other water people without a love story. The 1994 film *The Secret of Roan Inish* is a great example. It's the story of a girl whose family has mysterious connections to selkies, the seal people.

The movie takes place in Ireland. Fiona's baby brother disappeared as a child, lost at sea. When Fiona learns about selkie legends from her grandparents, she decides that her brother must have been saved by these kindly water dwellers. To solve the mystery, she returns to Roan Inish, the island where she lived when her brother disappeared.

Another watery puzzle unfolds in *The Tail of Emily Windsnap*. This 2004 book, the first in a series by Liz Kessler, imagines the life of a regular girl who makes a shocking discovery about herself. Twelve-year-old Emily has never learned to swim. When her seventh-grade gym class hits the pool, her legs feel strange. Emily leaves the water, but before long, her curiosity draws her into the ocean. There her legs turn into a fish's tail. She's a mermaid!

Emily's nighttime swims help her make friends with another mermaid, Shona. Shona introduces her to the world that exists under the sea. But Emily still has a life on land as well, and now she has a secret to protect. Plus she has plenty of questions about merfolk, the father she's never known, and what all these changes will mean for her.

There's no doubt that storytellers and moviemakers will keep giving us new ways to think about and enjoy merfolk. These weird and sometimes dangerous creatures captured our imaginations thousands of years ago. And like the mermaid who captured you at the beginning of this book, they will never, ever let us go.

A Swimming Tale

An Australian woman has probably come as close as a person can to feeling like a mermaid. Nadya Vessey (*below*) lost both her legs as a child. She can walk with the help of artificial legs, which are called prosthetics. But she also swims—and she does so with a mermaid's tail.

Like Nadya's legs, her tail is a prosthetic. It was built by a company that creates costumes and special effects for movies. The tail is made of the material used in wet suits for deep-sea divers. It has a fake spine to give it shape, with a flat fin at the end. To swim, Nadya moves the tail up and down, much like a dolphin swims. (Most fish have a differently shaped tail, which they move from side to side.) The tail is beautifully painted by hand to look as if it's covered with scales. As Nadya glides through the water, she looks very much like a fairy-tale mermaid.

Selected Bibliography

Beck, Horace. *Folklore and the Sea*. Middletown, CT: Wesleyan University Press, 1973.

Bedell, J. M. Hildur. *Queen of the Elves, and Other Icelandic Legends*. Northampton, MA: Interlink Books, 2007.

Bondeson, Jan. *The Feejee Mermaid*. Ithaca, NY: Cornell University Press, 1999.

Briggs, Katherine M. *An Encyclopedia of Fairies: Hobgoblins, Brownies, Bogeys, and Other Supernatural Creatures*. New York: Pantheon Books, 1976.

Garry, Jane, and Hasan El-Shamy, eds. *Archetypes and Motifs in Folklore and Literature*. Armonk, NY: M. E. Sharpe, 2005.

Louis, Liliane Nérette. *When Night Falls, Kric! Krac!: Haitian Folktales*. Englewood, CO: Libraries Unlimited, 1999.

Rose, Carol. *Giants, Monsters, and Dragons*. New York: W. W. Norton & Company, 2001.

Slater, Candace. *Dance of the Dolphin*. Chicago: University of Chicago Press, 1994.

Telegraph Online. "Disabled Woman Given Mermaid Tail to Help Her Swim." *Telegraph.co.uk*. February 26, 2009. http://www.telegraph.co.uk/news/newstopics/howaboutthat/4839818/Disabled-woman-given-mermaid-tail-to-help-her-swim.html. (March 1, 2009).

University College, Cork. *Annals of the Four Masters. Corpus of Electronic Texts*. 2009. http://www.ucc.ie/celt/published/T100005A/index.html. (March 1, 2009).

Further Reading and Websites

Books

Dunmore, Helen. *Ingo.* New York: HarperCollins, 2006. When eleven-year-old Sapphire's father vanishes at sea, her heart is broken. She misses his songs and tales about Ingo, the underwater world of merfolk. Then Sapphire meets two young merfolk and discovers that Ingo is real. She begins to realize that her father's disappearance may have a great deal to do with her own deep connection to the world beneath the sea.

Hoffman, Alice. *Indigo.* New York: Scholastic, 2002. The author of *Aquamarine* returns with another fantasy about connections between humans and mysterious water dwellers. Thirteen-year-old Martha's best friends are the McGill brothers, who are nicknamed Trout and Eel because they have webbed skin between their fingers and toes. Trout and Eel long to be in the water, but the residents of Oak Grove dammed up the creek outside town after a terrible flood years ago. Can Martha help her friends understand who they are and why?

Jarrell, Randall. *The Animal Family.* New York: HarperCollins, 1996. This book was originally published in 1965 and won a Newbery Honor Award. A lonely hunter meets a mermaid, who slowly learns to trust him. These unlikely friends teach each other their languages. When the hunter finds a bear cub, a very unusual family is born. The famous illustrator Maurice Sendak drew ink pictures for this beloved story.

Johnson, Alaya. *The Goblin King.* Minneapolis: Graphic Universe, 2009. In this Twisted Journey book, you choose your own path through a fantastical tale set in the fairy realm. Selkies join other magical beings in an epic battle between the goblins and the elves.

Johnson, Gillian. *Thora: A Half-Mermaid Tale.* New York: HarperCollins, 2005. Thora has a mermaid mother and a human father. That means she must spend ten years at sea and then ten years on land. She's just completed her first decade on the ocean, where she lived in a houseboat under her mother's care. Now she must go to the village of Grimli and figure out how to fit in as a human. That won't be easy, since she has purple feet, scaly legs, and a blowhole on the top of her head!

King-Smith, Dick. *The Merman.* New York: Random House, 1999. The author of the famous pig story *Babe* and many other books tells a tale of merfolk and a human girl who becomes their friend and student. Zeta is a ten-year-old girl on vacation in Scotland. She meets a merman named Marinus who can talk to seals, speak French, and name the stars. Marinus is nearing the end of his life, but he finds a way for Zeta to remain in touch with merfolk forever.

Nesbit, Edith. *Wet Magic.* Gloucester, UK: Dodo Press, 2008. The four Desmond siblings have an unexpected adventure when they accidentally summon a mermaid during their seaside vacation. Things get tricky when the mermaid is captured by a circus and the Desmonds decide that they must rescue her before she dies. Originally written in 1913, *Wet Magic* is one of many classic fantasy books for kids by the famed E. Nesbit.

Saxton, Patricia. *The Book of Mermaids*. Summit, NJ: Shenanigan Books, 2006. What holidays do mermaids celebrate, and how? How do they have fun? What's mermaid language like? And what's the latest in mermaid fashion? If mermaids were real and someone wrote an encyclopedia about them, this fancifully illustrated book might be the result.

Websites

The Little Mermaid
http://disney.go.com/disneyvideos/animatedfilms/littlemermaid/home.html
Disney's official website for Ariel and her friends is packed with activities. Visitors can watch a trailer and clips from the movie or download wallpaper, icons, and a screensaver. Crafts include stencils, character masks, and mobiles.

Mythic Creatures: Dragons, Unicorns, and Mermaids
http://www.amnh.org/exhibitions/mythiccreatures/water/mermaids.php
The American Museum of Natural History created this website to go along with a traveling museum exhibit on many kinds of mythical beasts. The "Becoming Mermaids" section of the website tells of mermaids from throughout the world, including Mami Wata and many others. Viewers can also read the words of the English explorer Henry Hudson, who wrote about a mermaid his crew thought they spotted in 1608.

Strange Science: Forgeries and Frauds

http://www.strangescience.net/stfor2.htm

This unusual website describes cases in which scientists have goofed. Based on actual books and historical events, the entries bring to life mythical creatures that scientists believed to be real. The entry on the Feejee Mermaid shows how P. T. Barnum made a fortune in 1842 by putting the fake mermaid on display for a fee.

Index

About the Author

Shannon Knudsen has written books for young readers about elephants, mayors, the explorer Leif Eriksson, the reporter Nellie Bly, and many other topics. She lives with her cat and her dog in Tucson, Arizona. When she isn't writing, she likes to explore the desert and see how many of its plants and animals she can name.

Photo Acknowledgments

The images in this book are used with the permission of: The Art Archive/John Meek, p. 1; © Bill Hauser/Independent Picture Service, pp. 4, 10–11, 20, 28, 34; © National Gallery, London/Art Resource, NY, p. 6; © David Fleetham/Taxi/Getty Images, p. 7; © Reinhard Dirscherl/Visuals Unlimited, Inc., p. 9; The Art Archive/Bodleian Library Oxford, Bodley 764 folio 74v, p. 13; © David Lyons/Alamy, p. 14; © Photononstop/SuperStock, p. 15; © David Toase/Photodisc/Getty Images, p. 16; © Royal Academy of Arts, London, p. 18; © akg-images, p. 19; © Thony Belizaire/AFP/Getty Images, p. 22; © Mark Carwardine/Visuals Unlimited, Inc., p. 24; © Museum of East Asian Art, Bath, Great Britain/HIP/Art Resource, NY, p. 25; © HIP/Art Resource, NY, p. 25; The Granger Collection, New York, p. 26; © Black Star/Alamy, p. 27; M. Violante, p. 30; © The British Library/HIP/The Image Works, p. 31; © Presidents and Fellows Harvard University, Peabody Museum of Archaeology and Ethnology, 97-39-70/72853, p. 32; © David Chapman/Alamy, p. 33; © Rohan/Stone/Getty Images, p. 36; Courtesy Everett Collection, p. 37; TM & Copyright © 20th Century Fox Film Corp. All rights reserved/Everett Collection, p. 39; © Weta Workshop Ltd, Photographer: Steve Unwin, p. 41. All page backgrounds illustrated by © Bill Hauser/Independent Picture Service.

Front Cover: © Nicole Cardiff; © iStockphoto.com/Michelle Bennett (background).